Praise for *Benjamin E. Ma...*

"Dr. Benjamin Elijah Mays, best known as the inspiring mentor of Dr. Martin Luther King, Jr., emphasized the interrelationship between education, personal integrity and the struggle for social justice. It is hard to imagine an academic institute so adeptly embodying the essential teachings of Dr. Mays as the institute bearing his name envisioned and founded by Mr. Sadiq Ali in Hartford, Connecticut, in 1995. Over the years I have come to learn that it was not only the institute that embodied these essential teachings. The founder of the institute also embodies these teachings, personally and professionally. A major role of education in the Benjamin E. Mays Institute was to inspire social responsibility and social engagement for the student, the student's family, and the institute faculty. Making education a transformative process for the individual and the surrounding society makes one deserving of the title 'Mwalimu'—honored teacher—in Swahili. At this time of excess mortality and mass incarceration of young people in Black and Brown communities, I join many others in celebrating the completion of this urgently needed book on the Benjamin E. Mays Institute by my brother, colleague and honored teacher, Mwalimu Sadiq Ali."

—Randolph G. Potts, Ph.D., licensed clinical psychologist, fellow and diplomate in African Centered/Black Psychology. Recipient of the 2014 Bobby E. Wright Award by the Association of Black Psychologists. Author of "Dehumanization, paranoia and deadly police violence in Black communities," *Psych Discourse* (Winter 2014); "Rites of passage in prison settings: Interrupting rituals of mass incarceration," *Black Child Journal* (Summer 2013); and other works.

To Lori,
stay strong and keep
the faith

[signature]

Benjamin E. Mays Institute

"God consciousness, along with intellectualism,
establishes and sustains supreme integrity."

—Sadiq Ali

Benjamin E. Mays Institute

Educating Young Black Males

By Sadiq Ali

Founder of the Benjamin E. Mays Institute

BELLE ISLE BOOKS
www.belleislebooks.com

ISBN: 978-1-9399305-1-4
Library of Congress Control Number: 2015945091

Printed in the United States

Published by
BELLE ISLE BOOKS
www.belleislebooks.com

The premature passing of my former students,
James Moore, Asaph Schwapp and Darrell Lacross,
inspired me to write this book.

"My Lord, increase me in knowledge."

Holy Quran

Contents

Introduction

❧

An Education Revolution

Dr. Benjamin Elijah Mays was president of Morehouse College, an all-male institution in Atlanta, Georgia, from 1940–1967. Being an ordained minister as well as an educator, he was an influence and mentor to one the college's famous students, Dr. Martin Luther King Jr.

The Benjamin E. Mays Institute was a seventh and eighth grade all-male academy that was located within Lewis Fox Middle School of Hartford, Connecticut's, public school system. The academy existed from 1995, its inception year, until 2005. Throughout the latter chapters of this book, you will be made aware of the unfortunate but preventable demise of such a thriving educational institution for one hundred black males throughout the north end of Hartford, a section of the city that includes some of the nation's most impoverished communities, comprised predominately of black people.

Hartford, Connecticut's, north end communities reflected many impoverished inner city neighborhoods in 1994. During that year, the schools in the city performed the poorest on the state standardized Connecticut Mastery Test compared to other cities and towns in the state. This outcome was consistent with previous years as well. Males tested the lowest throughout all schools in the city. In fact, the high school graduation rate among boys was supremely dismal. In saying that a little over a quarter of the males graduated each year is providing a generous figure.

As a reflection of the remainder of black males in America, one of every three black males was involved in the penal system in 1994. There were more black males going to prison in Hartford than being enrolled in college.

Hartford experienced its greatest number of homicides ever in 1994. Due to the tremendous dropout and unemployment rates among young black men, gang violence reached its height of activity and dominance during that year in particular. Gang wars, primarily over control of turf for dealing drugs, led to the murders of many black boys and young men, including a few of my former students.

In December of 1994, an eighth grader was murdered due to the gang wars. He was not my student; however, he was a neighbor and friend of some of my male students. The day following the murder, many of my students ran to me in fear that they were going to lose their lives in the same fashion. At that moment, I realized that an innovative approach to educating these young men needed to be created. I wasn't sure what, but this approach had to be relevant in making those low self-esteemed boys proud of themselves and dissolve their existing fears and hopelessness.

After much reflection and meditation over the weekend, that Monday, I called a meeting with all of my boys to obtain insight into the rationale of the overwhelming gang violence. One young man responded by indicating—in his own jargon, of course—that extreme illiteracy amongst black males had created unemployment and hopelessness. They felt they had the ability for nothing else but to sell drugs. I then inquired for possible solutions. That same young man suggested that schools be created that would focus on black males only because traditional schools failed to do so.

The following day, I met with my assistant principal, Sylvia Hooker, to discuss that conversation, and we explored the concerns and thought processes of potentially creating an all-male education program. Ms. Hooker is an extraordinary, visionary educator. She inspired me to address the male failure rate in the city of Hartford through innovative pedagogy to obtain success. Throughout my process, she served as my consultant and mentor and was a dear friend.

Ms. Hooker recommended that I research existing all-male educational institutions in communities similar to our to obtain cognizance of their educational methodologies and rationales. I studied three in Detroit, Michigan: Malcolm X, Marcus Garvey and Paul Robeson academies. In doing so, I learned that their focus was African-centered instruction with a strong mentoring component. I had also identified that Project 2000, the all-male institution founded by Dr. Spencer Holland, located on the campus of Morgan State

University in Baltimore, Maryland, concentrated on math development. I theorized that Project 2000 envisioned the significance of the developmental skills in science, technology, engineering and math (S.T.E.M.), a pedagogy before its time. Project 2000 also established a strong mentoring component.

Ms. Hooker provided me with the guidance and support to initiate a mentoring program for my male students effective mid-December of 1994. This program's services were two-fold: 1) to instill character development in male students through the leadership and role modeling by strong, positive men from the community, and 2) to serve as a pilot for a potential all-male academy.

The mentors consistently came into the school to meet with their mentees, inquiring about academic efforts and citizenship that was provided by staff. They supplied tutoring for boys who struggled academically. The mentors also conducted workshops for students on issues that affected and influenced young black males. These methodologies were extremely vital components to the improvement of self-esteem and the feeling of hopelessness. My students would be taught to identify obstacles and become successful by men who had lived their lives, and who had thrived despite similar horrific conditions.

Last, the mentors provided chaperoning on field excursions. One such experience was attending the Boys Choir of Harlem concert at Southern Connecticut State University. Ms. Hooker arranged the experience and provided bus transportation. As a result of observing the choir, my students realized that young black males can be remarkable, no matter their economic or social situations. This observation had a profoundly positive impact on my boys.

The program also provided study periods that were separate for the female population. The separation proved to provide greater concentration on homework.

The mentoring program proved to be highly successful. Academic efforts increased, resulting in the improvement of grades. Positive citizenship increased. Suspensions, office referrals and detentions decreased dramatically. The boys engaged in community service programs to assist neighbors in need. They began exhibiting positive efforts in their instruction and conduct. Students in the elementary schools gained a sense of awareness of the boys' new image. They, too, looked forward to being part of such an impactful program.

Due to the success of the program, Ms. Hooker and I determined that it was time for us to propose to the Hartford Public Schools superintendent and the board of education the concept of having an all-male academy for the next school year (1995–1996), making it the first ever in the Connecticut public school system and one of the few existing in the nation at the time.

In May of 1995, Ms. Hooker and I gathered some supporters to explain the rationale and significance of an all-male academy to central office administrators and board members, with the ultimate goal of gaining support and funding. Ms. Hooker and I, along with Ginger Whitaker, an English teacher and colleague of mine, explained to the administrators the pedagogical identifications and rationale for such an academy. The mentors described the effectiveness in character development, and girls from the school presented testimony to the improvements of the boys' academic efforts and citizenship in class and community. For example, the girls made the audience aware of the boys' improved reading and writing focus and skills, the understanding of algebraic operations and their new interest in science.

Later, school officials informed us that they needed to research the legal ramifications of allowing an all-male academy in public schools first before approval. Of course, the district feared the potential of a discriminatory lawsuit (unequal educational opportunities for girls).

Days following our proposal presentation at the board of education, Ms. Hooker recommended "Benjamin E. Mays Institute" as the name for the all-male academy, to pay homage to Dr. Mays and Morehouse College. In anticipation and preparation for the district's denial of Mays Institute due to perceived unequal opportunities for females, Ms. Hooker wisely created a name for a possible future all-girls academy that would be compatible to Mays, the Mary McLeod Bethune Institute. Yes, Bethune was initiated at the start of the 1996 school year.

Prior to the closing of the 1994–95 school year, we had yet to receive approval from school officials on whether the Benjamin E. Mays Institute would exist come September of the new school year. However, I did receive upsetting yet proud news near the last day of school. Ms. Hooker, my beloved friend, had accepted a central office administrative position in the South for the upcoming school year. Even though I was happy for her, I realized that without my consultant available, I had to grow up quickly to master the implementation of an African-centered pedagogy for black males. Over the summer, I spent tremendous time studying the theories and implementation recommendations of African-centered educational experts Dr. Jawanza Kunjufu, the highly regarded black education consultant; Dr. Na'im Akbar, an educational psychology professor; Dr. Asa Hilliard, an educational psychology professor; and Dr. Maulana Karenga, African studies professor and founder of the African values concept Nguzo Saba. The studies of these authors, along with others, were essential in my development of this innovative approach to education.

In mid to late August, near the start of the 1995–1996 school year, Hartford Public Schools approved the proposal of the Benjamin E. Mays Institute. As one could imagine, this required tremendous scrambling to prepare and arrange for the initiation of one of Connecticut's pioneering innovative educational environments. School opened following Labor Day and even though I had received offers and recommendations to establish Mays within a multitude of other established schools, approval was given under the stipulation that Mays would be housed within Lewis Fox Middle School.

Prior to Labor Day, Mays' opening could have been halted when the National Organization of Women and the American Civil Liberties Union threatened lawsuits, indicating that Mays would exhibit discriminatory practices of unequal educational opportunities towards girls. To continue with the scheduled opening of Mays, N.O.W. insisted that girls be enrolled. The A.C.L.U. required that a compatible institution be provided for girls as well. Following a lengthy discussion and collaborative efforts between the two organizations, Hartford school officials and myself, an agreement was made that upon Mays' initiation, an all-female academy would be established the following school year (Mary McLeod Bethune Institute) and a female support program would immediately exist.

Stacy Epps, a Hartford Public Schools social worker, worked with Amos Smith to establish a successful mentoring initiative for Lewis Fox Middle School's girls. Epps and Smith used the Always On Saturday Program, an academic support, cultural and character development organization for Hartford youths, which Smith had founded. This program proved to be extremely vital in the piloting of Mary McCleod Bethune Institute.

On the first day of school in September of 1995, the Benjamin E. Mays Institute was opened for business, making it the first all-male educational institution in the Connecticut public school system and one of the few in the United States.

My wife, Janice Thomas-Brown, a veteran art teacher of Hartford Public Schools, designed Mays Institute's logo, which exhibited the large initials for Benjamin E. Mays Institute: B.E.M.I. Written in smaller text along each large letter were: Better Educated Men Incorporated. At the bottom of the logo, she wrote in even smaller text: Into a Society. Yes, Benjamin E. Mays Institute, Better Educated Men Incorporated Into a Society. That was us!

The Mays Institute received extraordinary media attention and coverage, both nationally and internationally, due to its initiation in Hartford Public Schools. For months, and on a daily basis, I communicated with those nationally who were inquiring about theories and rationales for the existence of the all-male education focus. I received telephone calls and interview requests from *The New York Times* and *The Washington Post*, as well as the *Hartford Courant*. In fact, CBS's Paris, France, affiliate came to Connecticut in 2002 to cover the dynamics of the academy. In September of 1995, four national issues attracted and engaged the black community: the O.J. Simpson trial, the Million Man March, the Sheff vs. O'Neill case in Connecticut (equal opportunities for education) and the Benjamin E. Mays Institute.

1

Staff

In order to thrive as a black all-male academy, designed to utilize innovative educational methodologies within a failing, impoverished and high-crime community, it was imperative that we obtain a staff suitable to meet the challenge. The students at hand, ages twelve to fourteen years old, were rambunctious and hardened. They were academically deficient and misguided and teaching them and holding their attention would be a stupendous task for anyone. Therefore, we knew we must find educators able and willing to face the obstacles accompanying the enrollment of such boys. No doubt, the Benjamin E. Mays Institute established such a staff.

The Mays Institute's staff was ideally suited to the task of establishing and maintaining challenging expectations, using innovative methods that would demand the best of the students as well as the staff. Our members possessed impressive backgrounds relevant to our objectives, and each person's character and personalities were suitably demanding—they had commanding presences that could hold each student's attention. All of us as staff members had extensive competitive athletic backgrounds, which were inevitably accompanied by mental determination, thus enabling us to establish exceptional classroom management abilities. Much of the staff had been brought up in similar communities and conditions as those of the students. The staff had effective methods for instilling aspirations in the students, for inspiring them to attain success, enabling them to thrive despite their problematic conditions. Our staff had substantial knowledge of societal dynamics, and we provided compassion to such a needy community.

Staff members were primarily recruited and hired by the administration, under the recommendations and advice of Doug McCrory, my colleague and right-hand man, and, of course, myself. However, the administration carried the primary responsibility for recruiting and hiring. This phenomenal new approach towards educating black males was very inspirational and important in the fight to save our endangered boys.

The spirit of the Million Man March also inspired applicants and transfers into Mays' teaching corp.

Throughout Mays' ten-year existence, staff membership varied, for several reasons. As a result of persistent difficulties, the superintendent removed the entire staff of Lewis Fox Middle School, including Mays' beloved assistant principal, Dr. Charles Groce. Some Mays teachers became administrators themselves, moving on to other locales. A few staff members decided to relocate. There were only a couple of teachers who were transferred to other teaching environments because they didn't work out with the academy.

This chapter identifies how the characteristics of the staff inspired and influenced the success of previously low-achieving students.

Dr. Charles Groce was the assistant principal of the Benjamin E. Mays Institute at its inception (the 1995 school year). Dr. Groce had played basketball at Winston-Salem State University during the early 1960s under the leadership of legendary coach Clarence "Big House" Gaines.

He later served in the United States Navy. Dr. Groce possessed profound leadership capacities for leading an entire community. His philosophical and theoretical approaches inspired me tremendously. He was the chief architect in Mays' pursuit of establishing charter school status in the year 2000. Dr. Groce's extraordinary insight on the afflictions and obstacles of black boys and young men served as a learning instrument for me in regards to administering innovative educational methodologies for the students of Mays. I've adopted him as my big brother. Even though Mays Institute flourished, Fox Middle School continued to decline. As I mentioned, the newly appointed superintendent of Hartford Public Schools, Patricia Daniels, decided to remove and replace the school's entire administrative staff, including Dr. Groce. Despite serious pleading from Mays staff and the community to keep Dr. Groce with the academy, Ms. Daniels refused our ardent request and replaced him.

Doug McCrory was one of our original math teachers. He also served as my partner in establishing Mays' endeavors. Mr. McCrory was a former basketball star for the University of Hartford during the 1980s. He was extremely active in the local chapter of the Omega Psi Phi Fraternity. His exceptional charisma was instrumental in obtaining community support for Mays. He was vital in the establishment of the academy's mentoring component. Mr. McCrory possessed acute awareness of the students' conditions and was responsible for producing the greatest standardized Connecticut Mastery Test scores in math in the Hartford Public Schools during the 1999 and 2000 school years. Mr. McCrory later became an assistant principal throughout the school district and a representative in Connecticut's General Assembly.

Ginger Whitaker was the academy's original English teacher. Ms. Whitaker had superb literacy teaching methodologies. Her no-nonsense approach instilled great critical writing and reading comprehension efforts in our students. She was also an established author.

Sheldon Neal replaced Dr. Groce as the assistant principal of Mays Institute. Mr. Neal was well-versed in scripture, yet extremely street smart. He was a remarkable teacher, demanding of the students and commanding their attention. He always instilled high expectations and never accepted excuses. Students never approached him without showing him the requisite respect. He possessed great wisdom and insight, which was beneficial to students as well as staff. He had high expectations of both students and staff. Excuses were not acceptable. He displayed the utmost respect for my professional and moralistic opinions. Not only was Mr. Neal my leader, but he also became a great friend.

Andrew Serrao's responsibility was as a special education teacher in another cluster, the school's individualized student bodies. He was instrumental in establishing our class-proctoring component, which was comprised of our mentors (more on mentors in Chapter 3). Mr. Serrao consistently involved his full-time special education male students in Mays' endeavors, making him one of the founding fathers of special education inclusion, before his time with this educational practice now common today. Mr. Serrao attended Cheyney State University, where he was a star in track and soccer. His street-smart characteristics enabled him to anticipate problems and solve them successfully. Mr. Serrao later became a special education coordinator and principal.

Troy Wortham was the Mays English teacher. Mr. Wortham was both a professional boxer and student while attending the University of Hartford. As a result, he obtained the nickname and fighting name "Schoolboy." He was an extremely successful welterweight fighter who has been inducted into the Connecticut Boxing Hall of Fame. Mr. Wortham also provided consultation and training for local professional and amateur boxers. His refusal to back down from students' potential foolishness instilled a continued peace and focus within the classroom.

Bob Gibson was our science teacher. He was a football player at Southern Connecticut State

University and was head football coach at Bloomfield (Connecticut) High School. I once heard a student describe Mr. Gibson as "The Black Hulk."

Ron Wilson, Mays' math teacher, was a Delaware State University football and track star. Mr. Wilson served time in the United States Marine Corps following college and joined the Windsor (Connecticut) Police Department prior to becoming a teacher. Mr. Wilson began teaching math at Windsor High School in 2008 and became the school's head track coach.

Mazekal Duncan served as Mays' science teacher. His tremendously impressive articulation and knowledge of black culture and societal rationales captivated students and staff alike.

Thomas Hardy became our special education teacher once inclusion became mandatory. He was the assistant basketball coach of Hartford (Connecticut) Public High School and cross-country coach of Weaver High School. His great sense of humor, insightfulness and attractive demeanor inspired even the most challenging students.

Greg Dublin became the Mays English teacher after Ginger Whitaker left, when she came to believe it was more appropriate for her to teach in the all-girls academy. Mr. Dublin's extreme knowledge of literacy development and his utmost persistence and insistence led to the school district's highest writing scores in the years of 1999 and 2000.

Beth Heath served as the Mays special education resource teacher prior to the inclusion mandate. Her supreme drive and determination, along with her demanding expectations and strong mother image, were responsible for many full-time special education students becoming part-time inclusion. As a result, many students exited out of the special education program.

Rich Botempo was our science teacher at one time. He was known as the "cool white dude," as described by many students as well as parents. Mr. Botempo kept a boa constrictor and tarantula in his classroom. These possessions captivated the attention of his students and inspired an interest in zoology and biology.

Judith Glover was our guidance counselor. Ms. Glover's tremendous wisdom and experience provided extraordinary leadership, not only for the students, but for staff as well. Her mother-like approaches allowed for all to feel completely comfortable in looking to her for consultation.

Lastly, there was myself, Sadiq Ali, history teacher and Mays' founder. I possess an extensive collegiate athletic and coaching background. In 1976, I was the University of Hartford basketball program's fourth all-time leading scorer and rebounder. As a result, I am enshrined in the school's athletic hall of fame. I utilized those characteristics, along with my deep spiritual values and structured upbringing, to maintain an atmosphere in my classroom that insisted students establish and meet high expectations. Students were expected to be diligent, persistent and moralistic. My students were also culturally aware and gained self-pride. I, too, am a product of one of Hartford's most impoverished communities, in the city's north end.

The impact and inspiration that this dynamic, powerful staff had is hardly surprising. Although the students faced some of the most challenging conditions in the country, the skills of the staff helped them overcome the obstacles. Our extensive backgrounds in athletics alone dispelled the "dumb jock" syndrome. This influence had great merit because so many Mays students had participated in athletic endeavors since second and third grade. Not until they were enrolled in Mays Institute did they ever receive acknowledgment that athletic and academic success coexisted. In fact, Mays' athletic boys were made aware of the rewards of the coexistence. Their teachers provided the living proof on a daily basis. It was just fine, in fact enticing, to be smart and tough.

As one student once put it, "We like our teachers not being punks." Of course, that young man told the world that his teachers succeeded in educating him because together they fought and conquered all of the ills society inflicted upon him.

2

෴

Pedagogy

In 1995, most students in Hartford's north end
suffered from insufficient literacy and math
skills. Of course, this contributed to students in the
Hartford school district consistently testing last on
the state's standardized Connecticut Mastery Test.
Another reason for such failure was Hartford students'
tremendously low self-esteem. My colleagues and I
were certain that rigorous instruction and African-
centered studies could counteract this problem,
ensuring student development in a community
that practically accepted and surrendered to low
achievement.

My instructional methodologies of reading
comprehension and writing skills through the
studies of geography and American history were
quite effective. In other words, I helped students
to improve their reading and writing skills through
the study of American history and culture. I focused
on vocabulary development, summarizing and
identifying main ideas and context clues, as well as
sustained reading. Critical writing was standard in
my instruction.

The students' efforts were inspired by the soft

melodies of jazz in the background. During such rigorous writing assignments, they would quite often listen to Miles Davis and John Coltrane. Under these two great jazz phenoms, my students engaged intensely, applying the domains of Bloom's Taxonomy—creating, evaluating, analyzing, applying, understanding and remembering—in enhancing their writing skills.

My teaching methods were intense and no-nonsense, with no class time wasted. I accepted no excuses from my students and set high expectations for all of them. I demanded my students' attention and cooperation at all times. Behavioral issues and I were on collision courses, and I won every time. Amazingly, Mays' structured management established a reputation within the community. Even though we taught seventh and eighth grade boys, students in third, fourth and fifth grades were aware of Mays staff. I was honored when each year my new seventh grade students told me that they had heard of me when they were in elementary school.

My colleagues taught math (pre-algebra, algebra and geometry), science (earth and physical) and English (literature and critical and creative writing). They, too, maintained rigorous instruction and tremendous classroom management. Because of their extensive athletic backgrounds, staff members insisted that students work intensely in their studies through regiment and obedience.

Extending the school day was an extremely necessary strategy in our instruction. It was mandatory that our lowest achievers attend classes after school to receive remedial support. During certain parts of the year, Lewis Fox Middle School offered remedial help on Saturdays as well. Of course, Mays staff took advantage of this time, insisting that our students who were in need must attend.

Lewis Fox Middle School offered special subjects (non-academic) that Mays students were required to take as well. These were physical education, art, music, industrial arts, home economics and computer literacy.

Mays staff and support resources designed studies outside of content (history, math, English and science), which developed, inspired and supported intellectual growth as well as character development in young black boys. These support studies integrated African-centered emphases, making the content relevant to our students' ancestry and current heritages, thus creating conscientious students.

Nguzo Saba

As mentioned in the introduction, Dr. Mualana Karenga, African studies professor, created the African values concept. Mays Institute adopted all of its characteristics to instill in our students a sense of pride and a knowledge of ancestral heritage and to further their character development. The precepts of Dr. Karenga's concept included:

Umoja (Unity): Every Wednesday, Mays Institute practiced Umoja Day, in which students were required to dress in a white dress shirt, dress slacks, a belt, a necktie and dress shoes. This form of attire served two purposes: it inspired unity within the student body and gave the students an awareness of expected attire for professional employment.

Ujima (Collective Work and Responsibility): The efforts of Mays' student council (Ujima Caucus) and their participation in the Greater Hartford National Association for the Advancement of Colored People (NAACP) were remarkable. The student group met often with representatives of the civil rights organization to collaborate on addressing community needs and issues.

Kujichagulia (Self-Determination): Mays student editors and writers for the academy's newspaper (*Kujichagulia Publishers*) wore this label proudly.

Ujamma (Collective Economics): Mays adopted this characteristic as the academy's efforts in unified fundraising for off-campus study excursions and college orientation and preparation travel expenses (more on these later in this chapter).

Nia (Purpose): Nia encouraged the students to realize the rationales and significance of collegiate preparation, professional employment and involvement in community development.

Kuumba (Creativity): Mays students were quite expressive in their created works for our rite-of-passage program and poetic efforts (mentioned later in the chapter).

Imani (Faith): Students of Mays were inspired to believe in and trust the efforts of their ancestors, parents and teachers towards their development.

MA'AT

This ancient Egyptian values concept practiced by Mays students had tremendous impact on their character development. I've applied the concept following my studies of educational psychology professor Dr. Asa Hilliard's teachings (mentioned in the introduction).

Truth: Mays students were encouraged to practice honesty.

Balance: Our students were made aware that being well rounded had beneficial factors.

Order: Having organization and realizing proper perspective allowed students to value education.

Reciprocity: Our staff insisted that students exhibit gratitude towards those engaged in their developmental processes.

Righteousness: Students were expected to practice strong moral values.

Justice: Mays students were convinced to value conviction over popularity.

Harmony: Unification was taught and always expected. This expectation encouraged students to obtain and establish fellowship, peace and mutual support.

Rite of Passage

This values concept inspired the students to prepare for manhood through an African-centered perspective. Our program was taught by Lee Aca Thompson, rite-of-passage and dance instructor for The Artists Collective, Inc., one of the nation's leading cultural centers. This magnificent institution was founded and established by the late great jazz artist Jackie McLean. Students studied expectations, morals, philosophies and African history, as well as the continent's diaspora. They also studied traditional African dancing and drumming throughout the rite-of-passage sessions. These skills were exhibited during The Artists Collective's annual Yaboo ceremony, an annual event that celebrates participating youngsters' new maturational development.

Sankofa

This African values system taught students to study the past to understand the present and prepare for the future. Quite often, we would reflect on the histories, biographies and quotes of historic black figures to guide us through challenges. Examples:

"If you cannot read, it is going to be difficult to realize dreams." — Booker T. Washington

"Young man, find your ideal. And when you find it, bow down to it as though it is the very God." — Benjamin E. Mays

"If there is no struggle, there is no progress." — Frederick Douglass

"A life is not important except for the impact it has on other lives." — Jackie Robinson

"The future belongs to those who prepare for it today." — El Hajj Malik Shabazz (Malcolm X)

"I've helped hundreds of slaves escape. I could have helped thousands more had they realized that they were slaves." — Harriet Tubman

Staff and students would reminisce on taught black historical events that provided current and future relevance and explanations. The students learned of the accomplishments of ancient Egypt, the universities of Timbuktu, the kingdoms of pre-slavery West Africa (Ghana, Mali and Songhai), the slave trade and the institution of slavery, Reconstruction, Jim Crow and the Civil Rights and Black Power movements as well as today's issues that affect and influence black America.

Pan Africanism

Our students were taught to support the ideologies of all people of African descent unifying to improve our educational, social, political and economic endeavors. This was vital for Mays students to realize because many of our students were from Puerto Rico, Jamaica, Cuba, Haiti, Virgin Islands and, of course, the United States. It was significant that they understood and supported solidarity, for such efforts educated and inspired their community. Readings and documentaries from Marcus Garvey, W.E.B. DuBois and Malcolm X were our primary sources of studies.

Poetry

The students of Mays were strongly encouraged to express their knowledge of black ancestry and heritage. The creation of poems was a significant aspect of this. For inspiration, some of our greatest poets studied excerpts from poems by the famous black poetic group, The Last Poets. Students performed their creations in front of parents, classmates, school officials and high school students. Of course, their efforts received rave reviews. Lamont Aidoo, Orane McMayo, Anthony Daly and David Milton received remarkable accolades from community leaders and city officials for their powerful poetic performances.

Black History Conferences

Each year during the month of February, the Benjamin E. Mays Institute would conduct a black history conference. The conferences reflected issues that affected and influenced the impact of the black community. Participants consisted primarily of students, staff and social science intellectuals from throughout the nation who supported Mays' efforts. The conferences were held at Capital Community College (Hartford) and The Artists Collective, Inc. They were comprised of lectures, workshops and students' poetic expressions. Book vendors were on hand.

Mays organized and established the academy's most profound and impactful conference in February of the year 2000. Held at The Artists Collective, the conference theme was "Education for Liberation." At the start of the conference, Leonard Epps, who was then the history teacher of Weaver High School (Hartford), asked for the support of our ancestors through playing the African drum. Following Mr. Epps' performance, I provided an invocation by reciting the first chapter of the Holy Quran, Al-Fatiha, in Arabic then in English translation. After my prayer, Dr. Charles Groce and Dr. Dianne Diakité, at the time a theology professor at the College of the Holy Cross in Worcester, Massachusetts, prepared the participants and audience for the rationale and necessity of the conference's theme. The workshops immediately began after Dr. Groce's and Dr. Diakité's eloquent advisory and consultation. All workshops scheduled for the day were based upon African-centered educational approaches and effectiveness. Capital Community College physics professor Patton Duncan, along with his brother, Mazekal Duncan, Mays' science teacher, and math teacher Troy Wortham, conducted their workshop on science, math and MA'AT relevance.

Several influential women collaborated to share their insights on African-American women. Presenters were Dr. Lisa Delpit, chairperson of the Benjamin E. Mays Department of Education at Georgia State University, director of Atlanta's Center for Urban Educational Excellence and author of *Other People's Children: Cultural Conflict in the Classroom*; Dr. Diakité; Ms. Ida Terry, director of addiction services at Osborn Prison in Enfield, Connecticut; and Lucinda Canty, registered nurse in the Hartford area.

Dr. Gail Waldu, music professor of Trinity College (Hartford), and her students provided insight reflective of their workshop's title, "Rap, Hip Hop and Jazz: Music and Education for Liberation."

Dr. Groce and Dr. Randy Potts, clinical psychologist, then a psychology professor of the College of the Holy Cross and former professor of the University of Hartford as well as a supremely vital and integral force in the development of the Benjamin E. Mays Institute, conducted a high-powered workshop on ancestry reflection on education, social and economic developments. Their presentation instilled influential Sankofa values.

Lastly, Mr. Doug McCrory, Mr. Leonard Epps and I described the methodologies and relevance of African-centered education as it applied to the students of the Benjamin E. Mays Institute and the male students at Weaver High School.

During lunch period, participants could shop with the vendors while The Artists Collective students provided entertainment, including African dancing and drumming. The performers included many former Mays students.

Following lunch, Dr. Delpit delivered a lecture on her description and insight of the conference's theme. She also identified potential challenges staff would face from adversaries and skeptics in attempting African-centered pedagogy.

In concluding the conference, Mays students performed poetry and quotes reflecting the Sankofa concept. They recited their own creations, which were reflective and relevant to the works of Dr. Martin Luther King, Malcolm X, Frederick Douglass, Marcus Garvey, Dr. Benjamin Mays, Kwame Ture (Stokely Carmichael), Jamil Abdul Al-Amin (H. Rap Brown) and The Last Poets.

The conference had a tremendous impact on the students' continued consciousness of pride, self-awareness and conscientiousness.

Amistad Motion Picture Fundraiser

The great motion picture *Amistad* was released in movie theaters in December of the year 1997. On December 10 of that year, the Benjamin E. Mays Institute collaborated with the Muhammad Islamic Center of Greater Hartford, renting out a Showcase theater in East Hartford, Connecticut, to conduct a fundraiser film viewing. Nearly three hundred people purchased tickets from both organizations. Prior to viewing the film, the audience was provided a preview of the historical Amistad event by a history professor from Howard University.

Of course, the film viewing and overall fundraising event had a great impression and effect on Mays students' acknowledgement of their ancestry and heritage.

Off-Campus Studies

To extend the impact of our educational efforts, Mays staff created a methodology that provided instruction and knowledge outside of the school. I labeled this methodology "off-campus studies." At various learning environments, our students were responsible for primarily observing, utilizing inquisitiveness, analyzing and evaluating assigned items as previously instructed by staff. They were also provided lectures by site staff and documentary films observations as well. Such places of study and the topic included:

- The Metropolitan Museum of Art in New York City: studies of Egyptian and European art

- American Museum of Natural History, New York City: studies of ancient human and animal life
- Guggenheim Museum in New York City: studies of art that possess historical relevance
- Sony Wonder Technology Lab in New York City: instructional demonstrations of modern and futuristic technical task instruments
- African Art Studio Museum, a small, independent museum in Brooklyn, New York: encouraging students to understand and identify their relevance to the African continent
- Schomburg Center for Research in Black Culture in Harlem, New York: studies of great black literature and historical figures and events
- African Burial Ground in New York City: lessons on the strategic location and rationale of such a secret burial site
- Springfield Science Museum in Massachusetts: studies of the solar system, utilizing the museum's planetarium
- Harlem Renaissance exhibit at Trinity College in Hartford, Connecticut: studying those who impacted this integral aspect of black culture
- Joseloff Gallery of the University of Hartford: instructional seminar on American history by an art professor of the university
- Phillis Wheatley play at Cigna, Inc. in West Hartford, Connecticut: the portrayal of

this poetic slave instilled further pride and consciousness in Mays students

- Million Family March: on October 16, 2000, students, staff and parents attended this historic event in Washington, D.C. The spirit and identification of family values were such magnificent influences. This trip was in collaboration with Imani, Trinity College's black student union.

Forums

Each year, The Benjamin E. Mays Institute conducted forums with themes focused upon recent events impacting the communities of black America. During early spring in 1999, a Hartford police officer shot and killed a fifteen-year-old black boy named Aquan Salmon. Naturally, the community was in an uproar. In fact, the killing had a profound effect on Mays students. Aquan was a friend to many. He had played midget football with and against quite a few of our students. Distraught as well as fearful of being potential victims of such a disturbing act themselves, Mays boys were in search of reasons for the killing and solutions to the problems the young man's death revealed.

In 1999, staff and male supporters of the Benjamin E. Mays Institute established a forum to address the killing. We worked in collaboration with the Alliance of Muslim leadership, a male organization of the Muhammad Islamic Center of Greater Hartford, another affiliate of mine. The date selected for the forum was May 19, in honor of the birthday of Malcolm X. The forum served not only Mays students, but all male students of Lewis Fox Middle School.

The forum was facilitated by Abdul Rahman Muhammad, who was then senior vice president of the Village of Family and Children, a family outreach institution. At that time, Mr. Muhammad also served as president of the Greater Hartford Alliance of Black Social Workers. At the conclusion of the panel members' commentaries, Mr. Muhammad provided specific and detailed preventive measures in regards to potential conflicts with police. Dr. Potts identified the first book written by ancient Egyptian Ptahhotep four thousand years ago and how it illustrated ten ways to avoid becoming victims of violence. Imam (prayer leader) Qasim Sharief, at the time the resident imam of the Muhammad Islamic Center of Greater Hartford, announced that police socialization differs from that of the black community. Police not connected with the culture of the community receive misperceptions through the media and racist folklore. Imam Sharief also shared a verse from the Holy Quran that emphasizes, "Never will God change the conditions of a people until they change what is in themselves." He stressed that the black community, black men in particular, must strive for education enhancement and righteousness.

Lee Aca Thompson encouraged application of the Sankofa concept. He challenged the students to find the once-established greatness of our ancestors, to understand how that greatness dissipated and how education can retrieve it. Muhammad Ansari, president of Greater Hartford's National Association for the Advancement of Colored People (N.A.A.C.P) identified a verse from the Holy Quran that states, "Man plans, God plans and God is the best of planners." He stressed that the students should find their ideals, but include God in such aspirations. He encouraged the students to study the American Constitution and aspire to become politicians and law enforcement agents.

Martin Torres, a parent of Mays Institute and security officer at Trinity College (Hartford), urged students to educate themselves in impacting social ills then let their voices be heard. He conveyed to the students the need to inspire themselves and others and insist that their parents lead in obtaining these values. Mr. Torres also recommended that the students study the elders who survived and thrived throughout the Civil Rights era, learning their strategic plans.

John Goffe, a student of Weaver High School and a member of the school's Society of Black Brotherhood, an organization founded by Leonard Epps and enrolled with former Mays students, explained that the stereotyping the media portrays of young black males are, for the most part, learned from young black men producing such stereotypes. He insisted that young black men must clean up their images by overcoming education insufficiency, self-inflicted violence and immoral behaviors. They must dissolve this indoctrination.

Lastly, Mr. Epps asked the following questions: Why is everyone so afraid of young black men? Are they afraid that you will eventually figure things out and put things together? Once young black men do that, are they afraid that you will obtain and apply power? What will young black men do with that power? Will they be responsible for the development of their community? Following the elaboration on each question, Mr. Epps insisted that young black men must not only educate themselves for their own sake, but do so for those who follow in their footsteps. He closed by stating, "Men who move the world, the world cannot move!" Unification! Mr. Epps strongly urged that black males unify their efforts to become successful.

Psychology Club

Dr. Randy Potts designed and instructed this social-consciousness learning component of the Benjamin E. Mays Institute. Students studied psychological impacts on individuals and how they affect the entire black community. They became aware of the identifications of such indoctrinated methodologies implemented by the media and members of a capitalistic society to control a community's thought process. The students utilized the readings of "State of Emergency: We Must Save African American Males," by Dr. Jawanza Kunjufu; "Breaking the Chains of Psychological Slavery," by Dr. Na'im Akbar; and "SBA: Reawakening of the African Mind," by Dr. Asa Hilliard.

This study provided the students with insight into the conditions of inner city blacks and their impacts on the black community as a whole.

Summer School

The Mays staff were tremendously aware of the effect a ten-week summer vacation without academic instruction had on our students at the start of the new school year in September. Many of the skills that the students obtained by the conclusion of the previous year had to be reviewed, and in many cases, had to be retaught in September and October of the following year. Also, during the Mays years (1995–2005), the standardized Connecticut Mastery Test was given in October. Students' test results suffered due to the lengthy non-instructional summer.

Because of the staff concern, I researched existing summer programs that I felt were suitable to meet the needs of Mays students. Two programs were highly recommended and they both effectively served our students throughout their enrollments. One of these programs was the Connecticut Collegiate Awareness and Preparatory Program, which was led by Dr. Steve Perry. Under his direction, our students obtained significant literacy and numeracy skills while participating in his Connecticut Collegiate Awareness and Preparatory Program (ConnCAP). This extraordinary summer program was affiliated with Capital Community College of Hartford. Another influential program our students participated in for the summers was the Welcome Freedom Program of Trinity College (Hartford). Under the direction of Trinity student leader Afua Atta-Mensah, this black, student-led program guided students in Scholastic Aptitude Test preparatory skills (even though Mays students were seventh and eighth graders) as well as instructional studies anticipated for the upcoming school year.

College Orientation and Preparation

It was, of course, supremely vital that we inspired our students to become collegiate students, a standard operational procedure of Mays. Our focus was to not only expose students to college expectations, but encourage participation as well.

Dr. Potts orchestrated our students' participation in classes at both the University of Hartford and the College of the Holy Cross. I can recall getting a report from one student from the University of Hartford about a Mays student's participation (Aaron Codrington) in a history class. The professor asked her collegiate students, "What is Pan Africanism?" The class didn't respond, not knowing the answer, but Aaron boldly and confidently raised his hand and answered the question correctly. The class was extremely impressed. Another Mays student (Tyrone Burston) took a fifty-item test in a science class. He proudly obtained two items correct. This was a phenomenal quest for a seventh-grade boy engaging in a collegiate exam without ever being exposed to the class's subject matter. Again, the class was impressed. At the College of the Holy Cross, Dr. Potts arranged for our students to participate in a class called "Religious Philosophies of Malcolm X and Dr. Martin Luther King." Mays students, literally and in an impressive manner, took over the class in regards to providing their analyses on issues requested by the professor (Dr. Dianne Diakité).

Also at College of the Holy Cross, Dr. Potts conducted a seminar for Mays students on meeting the expectations of college rigor and socialization.

Dr. Gail Waldu directed visits and class participation at Trinity College. Science class exposure and collegiate students' endeavors were the focal points. Our students engaged in scientific experiments and shared social philosophies and theories with many of the college's black students at the Umoja House, the black student union center.

Sandra Riggins arranged for Mays students to attend workshops and classes at Yale and Harvard universities. While at Yale, the students were briefed on college preparatory while still in middle school. They also studied archeological life at the college's Peabody Museum. At Harvard, the students met with Dr. Henry Louis Gates. He engaged them in the studies of African-American history. Ms. Riggins arranged for a September 2001 visit to Princeton University, but the 9/11 attacks on the World Trade Center forced the superintendent of schools to cancel all field excursions.

Special Achievement Acknowledgements

Other than rewarding students with certificates for academic achievement, Mays staff created special accolades for students who were extraordinary. Such recognitions included:

Martin Luther King Jr. Highest Achievement Award
    – greatest academic achievement

Malcolm X Most Improvement Award
    – most improved student in academics
Booker T. Washington Leadership Award
    – display of greatest leadership efforts
Marcus Garvey Desire Award
    – greatest perseverance
W.E.B. DuBois Character Award
    – greatest improvement in character
    development
Frederick Douglass Literacy Development Award
    – greatest improvement or achievement
    in writing and reading skills on the
    standardized Connecticut Mastery Test
Mother Clara Hale Parent Award
    – parent who was most involved in Mays'
    efforts

Mays Students Out-Tested Lewis Fox Middle School and the Entire District

As a result of the Mays staff's rigorous instructional application, supplemental studies, summer school enrollment and mentoring program (which will be described in the next chapter), the students of the academy consistently out-tested all others on the Connecticut Mastery Test at Lewis Fox Middle School. In fact, in the year 1999, Mays outperformed Hartford's entire district in writing and math. That year, 63% percent of our students met goal in writing and 47% in math. No other schools in the district came close to the accomplishments of Mays.

3

Mentorship

In the introduction, I mentioned that throughout my research of existing all-male academies in 1994, I discovered that mentorship was a major component of the successes of those learning environments for black boys. The Benjamin E. Mays Institute adopted the utilization of this integral manpower. In fact, in 1995 in particular, the Million Man March created a desire for men to attach themselves to the efforts of community enhancement. Our mentorship served four purposes: 1) to play a significant part in the development of the students' character; 2) to assist in academic development and achievement; 3) to inspire collegiate enrollment; and 4) to build the desire for professional employment (career orientation and preparation).

Doug McCrory and I were responsible for the recruitment of professional employees to serve as mentors for the Benjamin E. Mays Institute. Those men were engaged in the fields of education, the corporate sector, law enforcement, and other public safety agencies, such as law, engineering, health and social work. Male college students were utilized as well. Dr. Randy Potts took charge of recruiting college mentors from the University of Hartford. He, along with Dr. Charles Groce, conducted mandatory seminars for our mentors, based upon strategic planning and the implementation of providing effective guidance in the development of the students of Mays. Dr. Groce devised an instrument that required mentors, on a weekly basis, to record hours spent with mentees, descriptions of the meetings and the results of the interactions. The instruments were submitted to Dr. Groce and Dr. Potts, who provided evaluation and consultation to the mentors.

Every other week, our professional employee mentors conducted workshops for our students on the development of their character. They also provided the students with insight on issues that affected and influenced black boys. Whether at their mentees' homes or at the school, the mentors provided tutoring. They also proctored classes and spent social time with their mentees; attended their sporting events; brought them on cultural awareness engagements; and even in some cases attended worship services with them. At least once each month, our students shadowed the mentors at their job sites. There, the students were responsible for observing their mentors' jobs, identifying the academic basis of those tasks and participating in small, doable tasks themselves.

At the University of Hartford, Dr. Potts arranged for the college mentors to provide academic oversight and escort the mentees to their college classes, where the Mays students observed and participated in instruction. One Mays student, with permission from his parent, spent a weekend on campus with his college mentee.

Besides being influenced by strong male educators, Mays students learned from the mentors, who were extremely instrumental in their educational, social and emotional development. The college mentors inspired a drive to focus on college attendance through current academic achievement. Their roles had a tremendous impact because they, compared to staff and professionally employed mentors, were closer to the age and generation of our students. The boys saw potential and hope for themselves mostly through the college students as a result. The professional employee mentors instilled a vision of career possibilities in the students, helping them to envision how they could develop successful qualities in their lives as adults. Both groups of mentors assisted staff in raising the aspirations of Mays boys, helping them to set their goals higher than other city youth.

Benjamin E. Mays Institute

Umoja (unification) Day

Ali's intense and no-nonsense history class

Men of Distinction awardees

Members of Sadiq Ali's history class

4

Support and Resources

The Benjamin E. Mays Institute was never provided with financial support from Hartford Public Schools to establish its separate innovative and reformative educational identity. I became quite aware that in order for Mays to flourish, we would have to become self-sufficient, perhaps obtaining support from recruited well-wishers.

Mr. McCrory, Dr. Groce, Dr. Potts and I continued our search for donors to the Mays Institute. We were blessed to associate with a number of extremely dedicated people, along with their organizations, to support our cause.

Many other people supported the work of Mays Institute in ways that went beyond finances.

First, I must emphasize that Dr. Potts was our number one supporter and resource. As previously mentioned, he taught the Mays Psychology Club sessions. He collaborated with Dr. Groce in conducting seminars for our mentors. Dr. Potts orchestrated our mentoring component on the campus of the University of Hartford and the visit-and-participation program at the College of the Holy Cross. He was also supremely instrumental in arranging and incorporating our successful Black History Month programs. He played an integral role in Mays applying for charter school status. An extremely huge portion of our success was due to Dr. Potts' efforts and his commitment to the Benjamin E. Mays Institute.

Mudarris Jihad and Leonard Epps, history teachers at Weaver High School, designed and implemented a high school extended program reflective of the pedagogy of the Benjamin E. Mays Institute. Their profound influence on Mays' former students enrolled at Weaver High instilled faith in parents and the entire community of Weaver. This helped dispel the negative image of the tremendously high failure rate of its male students.

It was extremely challenging attempting to recruit students for an all-male academy. Boys were quite often fed false preconceived notions and rumors of enrolling in such from their peers and others in their communities. Jealousy, envy, fear and ignorance were the culprits. Jay Gutierrez and Gregory Martin, two teachers from Annie Fisher and Mark Twain elementary schools, provided tremendous efforts in assisting us in recruitment tasks. Their connections and influences on the boys of their schools and their families and community as a whole supplied the rationales and significance of the all-male concept, thus easing the burden of recruitment.

Percy Christian headed an organization of black corporate employees throughout the state of Connecticut. His colleagues served as a major component to our professional employee mentorship. Their professionalism, dedication and insight had profound impacts on Mays students. Mr. Christian's organization enlightened the students to professional employee approaches to tasks, as well as to the standards of professionalism. For example, the organization's members would escort their mentees to their various job sites, providing opportunities for observation and participation in doable activities, especially those requiring academic utilization. This engagement encouraged an awareness and confidence in the students in establishing themselves as future professional employees.

Dr. Gail Waldu was extremely influential in the relationship established between the Benjamin E. Mays Institute and Imani, the black student union of the Trinity College. She arranged for visits and participation at the college and involved our students in Imani's efforts and endeavors throughout the college and community. Mays and Imani students collaborated in readings that inspired discussions on both campuses, Trinity's and Lewis Fox Middle School. Imani's engagement had great effect on our students, guiding them in establishing vision for the preparations, expectations and standards of collegiate students.

Welcome Back Freedom was an affiliate organization of Imani. Led by director and founder Afua Atta-Mensah, the summer program provided Scholastic Aptitude Test preparations for Hartford's high school students. The organization skillfully instructed Mays boys in the test prep process along with teaching and tutoring in literacy development.

The Artists Collective assisted in instilling an extraordinary sense of cultural awareness and pride in Mays students. The organization's sponsored rite-of-passage program enlightened our boys to the influences of their ancestors through their endeavors and culture.

Archie Kidd was the founder and director of the Future Basketball Organization. Comprised of Mays boys, the team traveled extensively throughout the northeastern part of the country, not only playing basketball, but also engaging in instruction while visiting various cities. This methodology was designed to effectively connect athletics and academics. Between basketball games, the boys visited museums and other resources for study. Being the academic advisor of the organization, I assigned analytical and evaluative writings about their visits. Mr. Kidd's program made Mays' participating students realize how athletics and academics coexist.

Minister Michael Copeland's Sons of Thunder Coalition was established upon the spirit of the Million Man March. His organization provided competitive summer basketball for high school students throughout the state, conducted field excursions to professional basketball games and mentored at specific schools in Hartford's north end. This essential program allowed for Mays staff to track our participating former students' high school efforts and advancements towards college.

The Ray of Hope Foundation was founded by professional basketball player Ray Allen. His organization has created opportunities for many disadvantaged students in Hartford's schools, providing academic and social support. Quite often, our students participated in the many excursions that Mr. Allen's foundation donated. On an annual basis, we were treated to tickets for Milwaukee Bucks *and* Boston Celtics games in Boston, Massachusetts. Once, Mr. McCrory escorted three of our students to Chicago, Illinois, to attend a Bulls versus Bucks game and ate at Michael Jordan's restaurant, courtesy of the Ray of Hope Foundation.

The Always on Saturday Program supplied participating students with Saturday morning tutoring as well as social and cultural awareness workshops. This organization took our students on many field excursions and engaged them in recreational activities, too.

Dr. Steve Perry directed the Connecticut Collegiate Awareness Preparatory Program (ConnCAP). The Capital Community College-affiliated summer program provided students of the Benjamin E. Mays Institute with relevant academic instruction in preparation for the upcoming school year.

Sandra Riggins' dynamic efforts in our college orientation and preparation component inspired tremendous vision towards the students' collegiate aspirations. As a result of visiting the Ivy League schools, the idea of going there became more realistic or tangible for the students. Going to college—period—became more obtainable.

The Benjamin E. Mays Institute's Council of Directors served as the academy's consultants, resource development providers and community connectors. The group was comprised of educators, parents, health providers, community activists and professionals. Those members assisted in the recruitment of mentors and establishment of college relations as well as in fundraising and obtaining instructional provisions. This group was implemental in Mays' being approved as a state charter school (more to come on this topic).

Quite often, folks inquired about the amount of financial support we obtained from Hartford's Board of Education to establish such a successful educational environment. I had to make people well aware that Mays never received any kind of budget from Hartford Public Schools. Many indicated that no way an academy could thrive the way Mays did without a budget. Of course, I always responded by noting that Mays flourished due to its powerful staff, tremendously relevant and effective pedagogy and mentorship as well as the great support and the resources obtained and established.

5

Mays Boys in Demand

As previously mentioned, Mays students consistently outperformed the remainder of Lewis Fox Middle School and the entire district as well on the state standardized Connecticut Mastery Test. Our boys became the most academically, socially and culturally orientated males in the city of Hartford, and arguably, throughout the entire state as well.

As a result, the students of the Benjamin E. Mays Institute were highly recruited for high school by private, parochial, technical and magnet schools around Connecticut. It was quite common for me to receive phone calls from such inquiring about the potential enrollment of our boys into their institutions once they entered high school.

Our staff's intention was to enroll our boys into their neighborhood high school, Weaver High. Our theory was that as Weaver received and nurtured such students, the students would radically improve the conditions and reputation of the high school and entire community as a whole. In fact, our parents were concerned that their successful sons of Mays wouldn't obtain a quality education at Weaver. They conveyed to us that unless Weaver had a continued program practicing Mays' pedagogy, they weren't going to enroll their boys at that particular high school. They would do so at the inquiring private, parochial, technical and magnet schools instead.

I previously mentioned the Mays' extended program at Weaver High, which was established by Mudarris Jihad and Leonard Epps. Their extension supported and continued the efforts at Mays. A more conscientious boy arrived at Weaver—those enrolled in Mays. Of course, Mays boys flourished at the high school under the instruction and guidance of Mr. Jihad and Mr. Epps.

Unfortunately, those two great educators' efforts weren't supported by the high school's staff and administration (details will be provided later). As a result, Mays staff, at the insistence of our parents, began enrolling many the academy's students into some of Connecticut's most prestigious private and parochial schools. Additionally, many enrolled in some of the most effective state technical and district magnet schools. Quite a few of our students attended Watkinson and Kingswood Oxford Schools of West Hartford, Suffield Academy of Suffield and Pomfret School of Pomfret. Some enrolled at Northwest Catholic High School of West Hartford and East Catholic High School of Manchester. Others attended Cheney Technical High School of Manchester and A.I. Prince Technical High School of Hartford. Many also attended the Classical Magnet and the Sports and Medical Science Magnet schools of Hartford.

6

Autonomy Proposals and
Charter School Approval

Even though the Benjamin E. Mays Institute experienced tremendous success, the academy also faced many challenges as well while housed in Lewis Fox Middle School. Mays' organizational functional philosophies were completely different from the rest of the school. Dissension developed between the different student bodies and staff. Our students were often ridiculed for their single-gender environment, dress code and academic success. Quite often, the boys were called nerds and accused of wanting to be white. The school's staff insinuated that Mays staff was provided preferential treatment in student selections and class sizes. In actuality, in Mays' inception and with the approval of the school's administration, we established an application process and we created a model with class sizes of no more than 25 students. The Mays staff felt that the academy couldn't obtain the necessary attention needed from the school administration, which was focused on the entire school and its resources, relevant teacher in-services and budget. (I will cover the many festering conflicts and their impacts in the next chapter.)

In 1996, Mays staff and the Council of Directors entertained several options for the school: by separating itself within Lewis Fox Middle School to become its own entity; practicing autonomy while at the school; relocating to an accommodating neighborhood site; or eventually becoming its own school. Even once-superintendent of Hartford Public Schools Anthony Amato advised Doug McCrory and me that two different educational philosophies within one school couldn't coexist. He encouraged us to entertain relocating. This vision created enormous challenges, retribution and the unfortunate eventual demise of the Benjamin E. Mays Institute. (Again, more details in the next chapter.)

During the 1996–97 school year, we inquired about establishing Mays at an abandoned but well-kept building in one of Hartford's housing projects, Stowe Village. Prior to addressing our inquiry to the Hartford Housing Authority, parents of our Council of Directors discouraged such an endeavor. They were in great belief that Mays parents wouldn't support such an effort due to the location, since it was a rough community.

In 1998, Mr. McCrory and I met with the administration of the Northwest Boys Club of Hartford in pursuit of possibly relocating Mays to that location. Their organization was very excited about such an aspiration, but realized that the facility was not conducive to educating students. Separate spaces to serve as classrooms didn't exist, no cafeteria facility was on hand and restrooms were limited.

Sometime later, Mr. McCrory and I encouraged the administration of The Artists Collective to facilitate the Benjamin E. Mays Institute. Both parties shared the vision of the profound significance of establishing an all-male academy within one of the nation's leading cultural centers. Unfortunately, Hartford Public School officials failed to support such an extraordinary innovative endeavor. They declined our request, indicating that rental cost for Mays to be housed at the Collective would be too astronomical for the school system to financially support.

Superintendent Amato's chief of staff, Robert Henry, suggested we relocate within a remote area of a Hartford school that had an extremely small population. Unfortunately, no such space was available.

Our Council of Directors investigated the possibility of relocating within the Old Clark Street School, occupied by The Artists Collective prior to building their own facility. Our advisory board concluded, through professional evaluation, that the building would be too costly to renovate appropriately in a timely manner.

In 1999, Benjamin E. Mays Institute's staff and the Council of Directors applied to become a state charter school. That year, we were denied due to two other prior existing applicants being accommodated. However, in 2000, the state approved Mays with a charter school status. In the months that followed, we were informed that there would be no funds available for 2000 charter school awardees.

In 2002, Dr. Groce, Dr. Potts, Mr. McCrory, Troy Wortham and I considered making Mays a boarding school, inspired by such an established school in the

Washington, D.C. area. We had our eyes set on the old Oak Hill School for the Blind campus, located in Hartford. We even entertained approaching then-Hartford mayor Eddie Perez to assist us in this ambitious endeavor. We became discouraged when we were informed that more affluent pursuers of the facility had been previously considered.

Influenced by frustration due to the conflicting philosophies and ideologies of Fox Middle and Mays, Mr. McCrory and I were quite adamant that Mays could no longer exist under the unsuccessful cohabitating conditions. In fact, we strongly considered disbanding Mays because of the conflicts and disappointment. We shared our sentiment with the superintendent, Mr. Henry. He pleaded for us to avoid disbanding and suggested to the principal of the school that reconfigurations within the school should be made to accommodate Mays' request for isolation. Even though an isolated relocation within the school came into existence, we continued to be impacted by the school's conflicting operations. Our feverous efforts of isolation and relocation did not hinder Mays' tremendous suffering.

7

Conflicting Issues
Lead to Mays' Demise

As previously mentioned, the Benjamin E. Mays Institute tried adamantly to separate its pedagogical existence from the confines of Lewis Fox Middle School through the requests of isolation and practicing autonomy while within the school. The eventual allowed isolation didn't solve or dissolve the contrary philosophies of Mays and Fox Middle, though. Consequently, conflicting issues brewed rapidly, which unfortunately led to the demise of one of the nation's only existing all-male academies in a public school district.

Throughout Mays' existence (1995–2005), Hartford Public Schools experienced four different superintendents and Lewis Fox Middle School had four principals. During this time, the Benjamin E. Mays Institute established recognizable and cordial relations with each superintendent—unfortunately, though, with the exception of one. During Mays' early existence, even though the academy flourished, Lewis Fox Middle School did not. The school's standardized test scores were consistently low. Suspensions among students, in particular male students outside of

Mays, were high. The school's enrollment decreased, primarily because parents enrolled their children in magnet schools and participated in programs offering inner-city students educational opportunities at suburban schools. There were actual cries from many within the community to enable Mays to instruct the further existence of Fox Middle through takeover.

When Superintendent Patricia Daniels was hired by the school system, one of her first tasks was to dismantle and reassign the administrative staff of Fox Middle. This action created a tremendous concern for the Benjamin E. Mays Institute because the academy's vice principal, Dr. Charles Groce, was also being reassigned to another school. Dr. Groce served as my number one advisor and spiritual leader. He became a big brother to me. Losing him would have been detrimental to Mays. The staff, Council of Directors, students and parents of the Benjamin E. Mays Institute met with Ms. Daniels, pleading that she not reassign Dr. Groce because his absence would impact Mays' progress profoundly. Ms. Daniels refused our request and reassigned Dr. Groce anyway. His love, determination and commitment for the Benjamin E. Mays Institute continued to thrive, for he passionately served on our Council of Directors.

One principal after another established his or her personal philosophy and ideology at Lewis Fox Middle School. Each re-establishment required the participation of Mays, of course. Quite often, we were forced to abandon most of our pedagogy and methodologies to adhere to Fox Middle's board directives. Each new principal adopted specific instructional and behavioral modification strategies. Most were never in congruence with Mays' pedagogical philosophy. Instead, we were always directed to engage in the school's failing and disruptive endeavors.

For example, Fox Middle adopted a reading program requiring that all students of the school be assigned a teacher outside of their respective clusters. This occurred at a time when Mays had established isolation. The academy's staff pleaded with the administration to allow us to teach reading to our own students, keeping them within the confines of the academy. Our request was denied. This program was implemented first thing the following the morning. When our students arrived back at the academy, I detected that they had lost much of the determination and focus we had instilled in them. Their working habits became sloppy and some began taking on characteristics outside of those expected of Mays boys.

Mays conducted monthly parent meetings, which were always well attended. The school's parent meetings never were, though. In fact, the total number of people attending Mays' parent meetings was greater than Lewis Fox Middle's numbers. Actually, our parents practically never attended Fox Middle meetings because they indicated that Mays' meetings were relevant to the educational, cultural and social development of their children. They didn't find it necessary to attend Fox Middle's. That changed. The school's administration prohibited us from conducting isolated and separate meetings from the rest of the school. We were instructed to assign our parent meetings with the school instead and then break out into our separate meetings, like the other clusters, following the school's parent meetings. We attempted this, once. While there, I realized that most of the parents at the school's meeting were Mays parents. I began theorizing that Mays parents were being used to assist in pumping up the registered parent meeting attendances of the school. Our parents realized the same and thus refused to attend in the future. Unfortunately, our parent meetings came to an end.

Mays' pedagogy required our staff to study methodologies relevant and effective to the needs and aspects of black boys. We insisted on specific instruction and advisory. We urged school officials to contract out as consultants Dr. Jawanza Kujunfu, Dr. Na'im Akbar, and Dr. Asa Hilliard (previously mentioned in the introduction and chapter 2) to provide us with the appropriate in-services and professional development. Of course, such requests were denied. Instead, our staff received directives to attend those mandatory in-services assigned by the school and content departments heads. No doubt, these meetings had no impact on our staff's development to continue developing our boys. Wasted time instead!

Envious Fox Middle staff members constantly complained that their clusters were overpopulated while Mays served only 100 students (50 seventh graders and 50 eighth graders). As a result, one principal after another forced our staff to enroll boys who never applied to be in the all-male academy. These enrollees, quite often, caused disturbances due to being forced into an environment that required a dress code and held only single-gender classes. These distractions expended valuable staff time and energy and they had negative influences on the boys who were originally and voluntarily enrolled. I asked the school's administration to allow us to recruit boys from other clusters instead of the guidance counselors and administrative staff assigning them to us. That way, we would have enrolled those who wanted actual participation. This request was denied. I theorize that the rationale of the denial was based upon the other staff members' fear of losing their highest-achieving boys to the Benjamin E. Mays Institute. Quite often, school staff insinuated that Mays students' test scores were much better than everyone else's because we recruited the "elite" boys of Hartford's north end. In response, Dr. Randy Potts adamantly stressed, "Mays staff does not recruit the elite boys of the city's north end, but they do turn boys into the elites." Besides, at that time, all boys in Hartford's north end were at-risk and considered endangered. Who were these elites?

The school system began experimenting with school choice a few years prior to Mays' demise. This policy and practice allowed for students to attend schools outside of their communities. Oftentimes, without our consent, we were required to enroll boys assigned by school officials, at the request of their parents. Many times, those were students with tremendous behavioral issues. Obviously, they impeded our progress. This strategy by school officials made me wary that the Benjamin E. Mays Institute was to be utilized as a "dumping ground."

Even though Mudarris Jihad and Leonard Epps' extended Mays program lacked administrative support at Weaver High School (refer back to chapter 5), our efforts to utilize the academy to improve the academic, cultural and social conditions of high schools boys in Hartford were futile. We lost our vision of impacting the male student at Weaver High School through our potential contagious inspirations. As mentioned in chapter 1, the students admired the athletically inclined teachers, so these men became positive influences in the boys' lives. Mr. Jihad envisioned utilizing the Weaver boys' basketball program to inspire such improvements. He strategized that coaching Mays' former students, along with other boys formerly of Lewis Fox Middle, would help instill Mays' pedagogical philosophies on the team and thus influence other students who weren't basketball players. Thus, he envisioned that the athletes would help inspire the entire male population of the school. Numerous times, he applied to the available head coaching position. Each time, he was denied.

I attempted to implement Mr. Jihad's vision for Hartford Public High School's male population by applying for its boys' basketball head coaching position. That school, like Weaver, serviced students from Hartford's north end. Doug McCrory agreed to serve as the junior varsity coach, my assistant. If hired for the positions, we would have taught at

Mays throughout the school day, as we normally did, and coached Mays' former students as well as others who had not attended the academy after school hours. Even though Mays boys didn't reside in Hartford High's district, our effort was to inspire their enrollment into that school's Classical Magnet Academy. I must mention that I attended Hartford Public High School and was decorated as one of the school's leading basketball players from 1968–1972, then later made basketball history at the University of Hartford (refer back to chapter 1). The combination of connecting Mays boys with Hartford High and my celebrated history with the school, no doubt, would have been profound in inspiring male achievement in that school. I, like Mr. Jihad, was denied the coaching position.

Had Mr. Jihad and I been the head coaches of Weaver and Hartford's basketball teams, we would have, under the strategic methodological approaches and implementations of Mays' pedagogical philosophy, inspired the developmental conditions of most of the male population of Hartford's north end schools. The city had three public high schools at the time. Unfortunately, school officials and administrators didn't share our vision. Thus and still, the boys at both high schools continued their low-achieving characteristics. Many boys continued to drop out of school. College enrollment was extremely low. The incarceration rate continued to soar.

From 2002–2005, I began identifying a higher volume of students enrolling in Mays who possessed a variety of emotional disturbances. These behaviors were not of the usual ill-behaved students. Their severe anguishes and hostilities keenly caught my attention. I detected potential psychological issues. Dr. Potts once told me that many children from our community suffered from post-traumatic stress disorder, along with other emotional ailments. These children merely existed, having never been diagnosed. In some cases, their conditions were even misdiagnosed.

I asked three members of our Council of Directors—Dr. Derrick Gordon, psychology professor of Yale University, Dr. Stephen Fagbemi, psychology professor of Capital Community College and, of course, Dr. Potts—if there was something that they could possibly do to assist in this major concern. They offered to establish a counseling component to the Benjamin E. Mays Institute for those boys we felt needed such services. Not only were all three of the men college professors, but they were practicing clinical psychologists as well. Obviously, I had to obtain permission from the school's administration to establish this much-needed initiative. My request was denied. Administrators informed us that the three psychologists couldn't provide such services to our students because they were not their own agency. Even if there was merit to the denial, I did not see anyone else appropriately helping those boys. In fact, I venture to say that no one ever took the opportunity to obtain mental health care for them throughout their entire lives. But again, we were denied.

In 2003, Lewis Fox Middle School's administration decided to dissolve the special education cluster at the school and disperse those students throughout other clusters of the school (the initial stage of inclusion). They decided to enroll all of that former cluster's boys into the Benjamin E. Mays Institute—of course, without our consent. For the sake of inclusion, the most feasible and appropriate method of successfully including those students into Mays would have been for the administration to have consulted with Mays staff. First, had my advice been requested, I would have proposed in-servicing our staff, by instructors skilled and experienced in implementing inclusion into such an assertive, aggressive and rigorous pedagogy as that at Mays. Secondly, I would have urged educating those boys and their parents about the academy, informing them of the philosophy, pedagogy, structure, expectations and inclusion methodologies, all provided in a thorough presentation by our staff. Because these strategies weren't utilized, sadly, practically all of those boys struggled with the academy's dynamics.

Each spring, I would go out into Lewis Fox Middle School's feeder elementary schools (eight of them) to recruit sixth-grade males into becoming our seventh graders for the upcoming school year. My presentations were extremely strategic. Recruiting sixth grade boys for single-gender classes was a tough sell. Marketing had to possess extraordinary insight and rationale, and it had to be evidential, convincing and visionary. Prior to my presentations, sixth grade boys had no concept of the benefits of single gender education and its rationale. However, they had many preconceived notions of what they believed it would entail. It was my responsibility to encourage the boys to dream of successful futures through the participation of our academy. This strategy required a certain amount of wisdom and sociological and economic knowledge, as well as an enormous amount of faith. Once fifty boys, along with their parents, had responded through our application process, I submitted the list of enrollees to our guidance counselor for legal and appropriate placement prior to September.

Unfortunately, upon returning to school in September of 2004, I noticed that only half of our recruits were enrolled in the Benjamin E. Mays Institute. Each year, students scheduled to attend Lewis Fox Middle School decided to attend magnet schools instead. Mays experienced this as well. During that year, roughly twenty of our scheduled seventh graders did not show up. This was extremely unusual. They were replaced, though, without our staff's consent, with other students. Practically all of those replacements were immediate behavioral problems. Being assigned to single-gender classes unwillingly would automatically inspire severe rebellion. Based on these students' behaviors, I was able to use my experience with children to determine that they were not just rebellious, but they had a history of behavior issues. I decided, as a result, to research the school's seventh grade enrollment. In doing so, I identified that many of our recruits were assigned to other clusters instead. This act made me theorize that the school's administration and counseling staff replaced many of our recruits with incoming disruptive boys who never applied to the academy. I believe that they did this in order to salvage the entire school's teaching staff from having to take on the supreme challenges that those students would have exhibited. They were dumped into the academy instead, leaving it up to Mays staff to rehabilitate them.

This recruitment replacement stunt was the last straw for me. I began strategically arranging to separate myself from such atrocities by transferring the following year, but I determined to continue my innovative educational applications elsewhere until I retired in 2013.

If you recall from chapter 2, we, most significantly, enrolled Mays students in summer school. The Connecticut Collegiate Awareness and Preparatory Program (ConnCAP) was extremely vital in preparing our boys for the upcoming school year. Each year, its director, Dr. Steve Perry, attempted to recruit me to teach in the program for the summer. I always declined, due to enjoying my summers off. Well, one year, my son needed braces for his teeth. Our dental health plan didn't cover braces so I decided to come out of summer retirement to teach in the ConnCAP program.

That summer, 2003, was a time when I was becoming discouraged fighting through the struggles that the Benjamin E. Mays Institute faced consistently while at Lewis Fox Middle School. I strongly contemplated transferring elsewhere. On my first day at the summer program, I was immediately attracted to the dynamics of its educational environment and began developing a vision. I mentioned to Dr.

Perry, along with others, that we should create our own school, turn ConnCAP into a magnet school. Tremendous discussion followed. After valuable theorizing and philosophizing with a few of the staff who shared my vision, Dr. Perry agreed it was most appropriate that ConnCAP become a magnet school. Being an avid supporter of the pedagogy of the Benjamin E. Mays Institute and its extremely significant single-gender concept, Dr. Perry wanted to establish the magnet school as all-male as well. During the fall of 2004, he and I met with Connecticut Commissioner of Education Ted Sergi to consult on the initiation of such a school. One profound piece of advice that proved most important was his warning against a single-gender magnet school attempt at that time. He reminded us of the extraordinary fight I had to endure in 1995 when striving to initiate a single-gender educational environment. Dr. Perry followed Sergi's advice against forming a single-gender school. Instead, he created a school for male and female, but with single-gender classes.

In September of 2005, we opened up Capital Preparatory Magnet School. Of course, I transferred out of Lewis Fox Middle School over to Capital Prep, dissolving the Benjamin E. Mays Institute and taking my innovative educational methodologies to an educational institution that was tremendously supportive of my efforts. At Capital Prep, I continued my successful experience of teaching single-gender classes, both male and female. The Mays pedagogy that I carried over inspired my Capital Prep students to thrive tremendously, not only leading the city in standardized test scores but in college enrollment as well, once they graduated.

In the meantime, though, unfortunately, Lewis Fox Middle School continued its failing ways—low test scores and a high rate of behavioral issues. In fact, two years after my departure, the situation there had gotten so bad that the superintendent of schools decided to close the school and forced its staff to apply elsewhere. All along, I continued to thrive with my methodological efforts and applications!

Conclusion

A Dream Deferred and Resurrected

I envisioned the Benjamin E. Mays Institute eventually serving as a pre-K through twelfth grade school for boys. My intention was to utilize the school to initiate and sustain a black male intelligentsia movement, unleashing brilliant, collegiate-aspired and professionally employed men into Hartford's north end community. Those men would, thus, enlighten and uplift the community's citizens out of their dismal conditions.

Actually, my colleagues and I theorized and philosophized the potential of applying such an effort at Lewis Fox Middle School to serve as a pilot to the ultimate vision. In fact, during a meeting with Doug McCrory and me, Amato inquired about our theory and philosophy on how Lewis Fox Middle School could be saved. I suggested a portion of my vision—the pilot program—that indicated converting the entire school into the Benjamin E. Mays and Mary McCleod Bethune institutes, Bethune being the corresponding all-girls academy. (Refer back to the introduction). I mentioned that both academies would become grades six through eight as opposed to their usual seventh through eighth. I also recommended that all of Fox Middle's feeder elementary schools be converted to grades kindergarten through eighth grade rather than only up to grade six. That way, any sixth through eighth grader not recruited and enrolled into the two academies would stay at their respective elementary schools. This ambitious proposal was never initiated, but instead, both academies dissolved and Lewis Fox Middle School was shut down. Many of the north end elementary schools did eventually extend to grades seven and eight.

Why would Hartford allow for such a thriving all-male academy to fold when the nation's public school systems began initiating their own similar academies in attempts to salvage their failing male populations? In fact, I received numerous phone calls from educators across the country requesting consultation on young black and Latino male pedagogies in preparation for their initiation of all-male educational programs. Why was I able to consult with those who successfully established such academies and schools when I couldn't do so with my own school system? To this day, it baffles me!

Even though most of Mays' students prospered and obtained successful high school and collegiate careers, there were a few who impressed me tremendously. Lamont Aidoo (Dr. Lamont Aidoo) is a professor at Duke University. The late James Moore, a graduate of the United States Air Force Academy, specialized in high-volume emergency traffic control. The late Asaph Schwapp received a football scholarship to Notre Dame University. He was later drafted by the Dallas Cowboys of the National Football League. The late Darrell

Lacross, director of the Benjamin E. Mays Institute Kujichagulia Publishers student newspaper, had tremendous vision and strategic planning awareness in establishing the academy's newspaper. He was well before his time. Michael Anderson became a star basketball player at the University of Washington. On the eve of my retirement (June 2013), Andre and Anthony Virgo graduated from my daughter's college, Virginia State University.

Being the spiritual man that I am, I honestly believe that the Benjamin E. Mays Institute continues to exist through those who thrive because of its philosophies and successes. As I previously mentioned, I was consulted for the strategic planning and implementation of programs to educate black and Latino males. Of course, I simply referred each of them to the pedagogy and methodologies incorporated by the staff of the Benjamin E. Mays Institute. Elementary and secondary all-male schools began springing up in Chicago, New York City, Charlotte and other cities.

There are quite a few collegiate environments that adopted approaches towards improving the educational, social and cultural conditions of black males, too. They all have Benjamin E. Mays Institute written all over them. Florida A&M University (FAMU) established the Black Male College Explorers Program. This initiative's challenge is to intervene and prevent at-risk young males in grades seven to eleven from Tallahassee, Florida, as well as other nearby cities, from dropping out of school; to facilitate their admission into a school of higher learning; and to increase their chances of becoming college graduates through rigorous academic preparation, mentorship, learning excursions, and college and career orientation as well as through economic development. The University Systems of Georgia's African-American Male Initiative, developed in 2002, and the University of California at Los Angeles' Black Male Institute, begun in 2009, both serve the same purposes. In 2003, North Carolina A&T State University established the supreme initiative, as far as I am concerned: the Middle College, an all-male feeder high school located on the campus of the college.

On February 27, 2014, President Barack Obama unveiled his "My Brother's Keeper" initiative, a call-out to the efforts to improve educational, social and economic conditions of young black and Latino males nationwide. It all sounds so familiar. Rightfully so. They all are currently doing what Mays initiated and implemented nineteen years ago. Long live the Benjamin E. Mays Institute!

In conclusion, even though numerous educators— at the elementary, secondary and collegiate levels— are realizing the state of emergency of young black males and attempting to address the problem through educational, social, cultural and economic developments, I wish to propose effective strategic plans to ensure sustaining these developments, thus improving the black male existence.

There is no doubt in my mind that strong black men must be engaged in the educational and social developmental processes of young black males. When I indicate "strong," my reference is those who possess great moralistic values, who are tremendously conscientious with admirable convictions, integrity, keen cultural awareness and, most of all, are spiritually sound. Men of such will serve as role models having the most positive impact on black boys and young black men.

Educators, in particular black male educators, must inspire and recruit our young men to major in education prior to or once enrolled in college to study to become teachers. The profession is in tremendous need of black male educators. Our young men are not interested in being teachers. I theorize two reasons. One, throughout their school careers, they have witnessed the ill-mannered behaviors of students. This fearful behavior discourages the young men from wanting to become teachers who would have to deal with such fearful behavior. Second, the education profession isn't attractive and "cool" to young black college students. They envision instead working for investment and other corporate firms that provide wonderful window views, company cars and access to expense accounts. These characteristics also influence their preferred studies of law and engineering. The enthusiastic culture of high-level law enforcement is also attracting our young men to the criminal justice profession.

Education, too, must make itself attractive to young black men.

First, school officials and administrators must provide meaningful and impactful in-services and professional development programs relevant to young black men's cultural and professional collaborative existences. For example, stop forcing strong black male educators to be trained in behavior modification methodologies that are better suited for inexperienced, weaker educators, accommodating the classroom management and instructional applications deficiencies of their colleagues. Those of us who come from extensive athletic and spiritual backgrounds and possess strong cultural consciousness and have been cultivated in structured environments will already come to the table with impactful disciplinary methodologies and implementations. Instead, as I mentioned in chapter 7, school administrators should allow the likes of Dr. Jawanza Kunjufu, Dr. Na'im Akbar, relevant athletic coaches and educators, and experienced black male teachers to provide the in-service and professional development for these strong, experienced educators.

Second, school systems should value the presence and teaching styles of strong black male teachers. Do not expect their performances to be comparable to others, particularly if their results are potentially or already substantial. These male teachers will provide resemblance and familiarization, as students can see themselves in these men. The teachers will instruct towards black male learning styles. Black male teachers will demonstrate that success is possible, even without access to resources. Also, studies have shown that the presence of strong black male teachers deters suspensions, expulsions and special education enrollment.

Third, schools should inspire black male educators to take on leadership roles: in administration, coaching, professional development experts, mentors for students and staff, and so on. I've seen envious and fearful administrators who groom weaker teachers instead of supporting more effective staff members who can better address the needs of inner-city students.

Finally, administrators should stop utilizing black male teachers as "dumping ground" supervisors. The most significant role of the black male teacher would be in the elementary grades, even in preschool. Their presence and styles are extremely impressive, influential and sustaining to such youngsters. Instead, administrators currently seem to prefer these teachers teaching at the secondary levels, primarily for classroom control.

Black educators must cultivate future black male teachers while they are mere students, even at the elementary level. Experienced educators in particular can identify potential leadership qualities in youth. Black male teachers and administrators should take those students under their wings, providing them with the necessary attractions and experiences to inspire their interests. For consultation regarding strategic planning and implementation of these tasks, educators can reach out to Dr. Jawanza Kunjufu, Dr. Na'im Akbar and others of relevance who can suggest appropriate books and resources.

Middle College of North Carolina State University is an ideal example: a black all-male high school on a black college campus. I urge and challenge black male educators to strive to establish their own schools on college campuses. Autonomy, selective philosophies, pedagogies and methodologies would be at one's fingertips. In 2013, one hundred percent of the graduates of the Middle College got accepted into four-year colleges. Imagine—one hundred percent of your black male students enter four-year colleges! That's powerfully impressive. Imagine if we could establish all-male high schools on all other Historically Black Colleges and Universities, with the excess of those schools' resources easily available to the high schools' staff and students: mentoring, advanced facilities, curriculum influence, staff in-services and professional development, cultural development, college orientation and preparation, and advanced placement classes.

I urge colleges, HBCU's in particular, to institute the endeavors of the University Systems of Georgia's African-American Male Initiative. Much of their affiliated schools' focuses are to provide preventive and intervention initiatives to address the failure and attrition rate of freshmen males through summer remedial studies, school-year academic support services and character consciousness programs.

Besides cultivating and attracting black boys and young men into the teaching profession, black male educators must strategize to recruit those who are studying education while in college. This would be an extremely monumental task for educators in the North. I found that most black male college students who are preparing to become teachers are located in the South, particularly at the HBCU's. Recruiting those young men would take economic intervention because Northern cities' costs of living may serve as a hindering factor. Northern black educators should establish rapport and affiliations with businesses, corporations and affluent organizations that could perhaps provide affordable rent and housing for the newly hired young Southern teachers. Those resources could also provide workshops and seminars to the Southern staff members on salary utilization in both sections of the country. For example, Southern teachers based in the North could make their significant purchases when they return to the South. They would learn that their Northern salaries stretch tremendously when spent in the South. I've learned and continue experiencing this firsthand as I frequently travel from Connecticut to Virginia.

Black male educators must affiliate themselves with black male organizations to assist in the complete development and productivity of young black males. Fraternities, black male professional associations (including professional athletes), 100 Black Men of America, and so forth can, no doubt, serve vital roles in the pedagogy process. Such manpower would be the key component of tutoring, character development, career orientation and development, cultural recognition and pride, and economic consciousness.

I urge that those same black male organizations establish summer educational initiatives for young black males. The organizations' resources along with guidance from black male educators could result in institutions that provide remedial instruction, course preparation and character development for students. Because the role models in these organizations are financially successful, they can inspire young black males to develop conscientiousness and problem-solving skills.

Currently, I am serving on the Greater Opportunity II Board of Directors, comprised of corporate and business employees, community activists and religious leaders. Its focus is to resurrect the Greater Opportunity Program, a summer school initiative that was established in 1965 to provide remedial support and curriculum preparation for one hundred high school boys of Hartford, Connecticut, and New York, New York. The program, located at the Hotchkiss School in Lakeville, Connecticut, from 1965–1973, also provided mentorship, which was vital to the boys' character development as well as their social awareness.

It is wise that black male educators who are in pursuit of operating their own schools establish a cordial and working relationship with public school superintendents. Those educational leaders are a tremendous resource and potential supporters. Their political and corporate ties will enable them to address the challenges of establishing and sustaining a school. Superintendents need educational winners. The academic and social enhancements of the lowest-achieving students in America, black males, will, no doubt, be a win for everyone.

Black male educators, along with their supporting black male organizations, must be politically active. Sitting on school district boards of education and city and town councils and serving in state general assemblies will enable our visions of the striving and thriving of black male educational endeavors to be addressed politically and constitutionally as well as allow us to have access to law and decision-making insight, consultation and support.

Lastly, I find it to be extremely essential thus I strongly urge that all-male schools and programs initiated outside of the public school sector establish a strong spiritual identity. No doubt, acknowledging God throughout the school day will provide males with tremendous attributes of respect for both self and others as well as honor, determination, anticipated achievement, dignity, integrity, humility and modesty, while still instilling pride, responsibility, leadership and conscientiousness. My current role as seventh and eighth grade language arts and male rites-of-passage instructor at Tawheed Prep School in Richmond, Virginia, allows me to witness, experience and support males' extraordinary responses to their established Taqwa—God consciousness—and thus the cultivation of such characteristics. Tawheed Prep is an Islamic private school for sixth through twelfth graders.

Even though I received tremendous accolades for successfully establishing one of the nation's all-male academies within a public school system in 1995, the greatest acknowledgement I have received was when one college professor provided me with stupendous recognition by indicating that a college or university should distinguish my endeavors towards the educational enhancement of black males by untraditionally awarding me a doctorate in education. Man! What a wonderful gesture!

About the Author

Although officially retired from Hartford, (Connecticut) Public Schools, Sadiq Ali is currently a language arts and male rites-of-passage instructor at Tawheed Prep School in Richmond, Virginia. As of September 2015, he serves on the school's board of trustees and chairs its curriculum and instruction committee. He also serves on the Greater Opportunity II board of directors, established to resurrect Connecticut's all-boys summer school initiative. In addition to serving as an educational consultant, Ali leads discussions and workshops on academic achievement and education, including a workshop on supporting disabled African-American males in the public schools. He holds a bachelor of science in education from the University of Hartford and a master in science in education from Central Connecticut State University. In 1996, Ali was inducted into the colleges Alumni's Athletic Hall of Fame for high achievement in basketball.

To contact the author, write sadiq10501@yahoo.com or visit www.belleislebooks.com.